POLAR LIFE

by Kristin Cashore

PEARSON
Scott
Foresman

DK

What You Already Know

Every living thing has its own environment. The living and nonliving parts of an environment work together as an ecosystem. All of the same kind of living thing within an ecosystem form a population. All the populations within an ecosystem make a community.

Our Earth contains a lot of different ecosystems. Some of the most important ecosystems can be found in deserts, grasslands, the tundra, wetlands, and both fresh water and salt water.

pond ecosystem

Grasslands get little rain. Deserts receive even less. The tundra receives the least of all and has long, cold winters and short summers. Coniferous, broadleaf, and tropical forest trees make up some important forest ecosystems. Freshwater ecosystems include lakes, ponds, rivers, and streams. Salt water ecosystems are mainly in the oceans and salt marshes.

In this book you will learn about the polar ecosystem. Polar ecosystems are harsh. Their weather is always cold. You will read about how animals are adapted to the cold by having thick layers of fur and blubber. You will also learn about the animals that seasonally migrate to the poles in search of food. Finally, you will find out about the interesting breeding and hunting strategies that some polar animals use to deal with the cold.

Arctic wolf

Introduction

Have you ever spun a globe? Do you remember the North and South Poles?

The Arctic is the area at the top of the Earth, around the North Pole. It is mostly frozen water. This water is called the Arctic Ocean.

The Antarctic is the area at the bottom of the Earth, around the South Pole. Most of the Antarctic is taken up by a frozen land mass called Antarctica. The Antarctic Ocean surrounds Antarctica.

The polar bear is the Arctic's largest land animal.

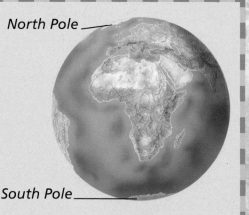

Map of the Poles

The geographic North Pole is the Earth's northernmost point. The geographic South Pole is the Earth's southernmost point.

North Pole

South Pole

Both the Arctic and the Antarctic have very long, very cold winters. Polar winters are dark, without sunlight. Polar summers are very brief. It is always light, and temperatures rise a little.

The polar regions may seem empty. But some animals live their whole lives there. Other animals come to feed during the summer. Even plants are part of these delicate polar ecosystems.

Penguins inhabit Antarctic lands and waters.

The Arctic contains rolling plains called tundra. Tundra is especially common in Arctic regions that border the Arctic Ocean, such as Greenland, parts of Siberia, and northeastern Canada. Permafrost lies beneath the tundra surface. This is soil that has remained frozen for a very long time. Permafrost lies under about one-fifth of Earth's land, including much of the Arctic.

During the summer season, the tundra surface above the permafrost becomes moist and marshy, creating wetlands in some areas. Moss, low shrubs, and flowering plants thrive during the tundra summer. Lichens grow on rocks and are widespread. Arctic plants survive almost anything.

It is summer on the tundra, and this Arctic fox's coat has changed color.

Antarctica is incredibly isolated. The world's stormiest ocean, the cold Southern Ocean, surrounds it on all sides. Antarctica's climate is harsh, with little precipitation. Scientists consider it the coldest desert on Earth!

Lichens, mosses, and algae make up most of the Antarctic's plant life. During summer, it is just warm enough for marine plants to multiply. Tiny, shrimplike animals called krill feed on these plants. The krill population swells throughout the Antarctic summer, forming swarms that cover as much as two hundred square miles. Eventually, whales and birds arrive to feast on the krill. There may not be many types of plants in the Antarctic, but life could not exist there without them!

The rosebay willowherb can be found on the Arctic tundra.

Antarctic lichen and mosses on rocks

Polar Bears

The polar bears of the Arctic are the world's largest land predators. An adult male polar bear can weigh up to fifteen hundred pounds! Polar bears search for food on land and in the sea. They cover an enormous territory while searching for the seals that they eat.

Polar bears are excellent swimmers and divers. They can swim for hours without rest. Their webbed forepaws help them to swim. Their blubber allows them to float.

Polar bears blend into their white landscape.

Snow Dens

Polar bear cubs are born in snow dens during November and December. The cubs stay in their dens for three months. Their mother protects and feeds them. The cubs in this picture are sheltered from the wind and hidden from predators. They stay warm by curling into a ball.

Polar bears are well adapted to their cold environment. The polar bear's white color blends in with the snow, so it can sneak up on prey. Fur and blubber retain heat, which keeps it warm.

Penguins

Penguins live in the Southern Hemisphere. They are flightless birds. Instead of flying, they slide along the ice and swim. Penguins can dive very deep and swim very fast. Their diet includes fish and krill.

Antarctic penguins range in height from about twenty inches to more than three feet. Their feathers are thick and waterproof. In addition, penguins have a thick layer of blubber.

Penguins breed in huge colonies. Right after laying her egg, the mother emperor penguin goes to sea to feed. The father balances the egg on his feet, covering it with a warm flap of skin.

Penguins are southern birds. They are never found in the Arctic.

Keeping Warm

Penguin chicks sometimes huddle together to protect themselves from the severe temperatures.

The father penguin stands in this position for two months, protecting the egg. The mother returns when the chick hatches. She feeds the chick regurgitated fish. Then the father goes to the sea to eat.

Penguins cannot fly, but they are excellent divers and swimmers.

11

Arctic Foxes

The Arctic fox roams the Arctic tundra. It stands about 25 to 30 cm tall, and weighs only 3 to 7 kg. It has a double layer of fur, small, furry ears, and short legs. Its thick foot-hair keeps it warm and helps it grip the ice. The fox's thick, white winter fur is shed in the summer for a thinner, brownish-gray coat.

The Arctic fox will eat almost anything, but it specializes in catching rodents. It listens for movement below the snow. When it hears a rodent, the fox jumps up and down to break through the snow and catch its prey. If there are too few rodents available, the Arctic fox will feed on the animal remains left behind by polar bears.

The Arctic fox sheds its heavy winter coat during the summer.

In the summer, Arctic foxes hunt alone and cover a small territory. They live in dens built into hills, cliffs, or riverbanks. Arctic foxes often take over abandoned squirrel burrows and enlarge them to meet their needs.

In winter, they must travel much farther in search of prey. Arctic foxes sleep in snow tunnels during winter, and live and hunt together in family groups. The female Arctic fox gives birth to an average of seven pups. Both parents help raise them. The pups leave the den by their third month.

Life in the Arctic is hard. Few Arctic foxes live past a year.

The fox's winter coat is heavy and warm.

Whales

The largest animals in the world include whales. Blue whales can be one hundred feet long! Whales are mammals, which means they must rise to the surface of the water to breathe. When they breathe, they push air through blowholes in the tops of their heads.

When a whale exhales, it releases a spray of water through its blowhole.

Whales have thick layers of blubber that keep them warm. Many types of whales migrate to the poles during summer to feed on the rich sea life.

Toothed whales eat fish, octopus, squid, and other sea animals.

The humpback whale sings many different songs.

Beluga whales migrate in groups called pods.

Other whales have baleen instead of teeth. Baleen looks like a brush with wide, flat bristles. Baleen strains krill and other small sea creatures into the whale's mouth.

Bowheads, belugas, and narwhals all travel to the Arctic to feed. The bowhead is a baleen whale with a mouth shaped like a bow. Belugas and narwhals are both toothed whales. Male narwhals have a long tusk, like a unicorn.

Baleen whales like the blue, fin, and humpback all migrate to the Antarctic. Toothed whales such as the orca whale and the sperm whale also swim the Antarctic seas. The orca whale eats penguins and seals. The sperm whale dives to below three thousand feet in search of squid.

Seals

Seals are excellent swimmers and divers. Their diet includes fish, squid, and crustaceans. Like whales, seals are mammals. They can stay under water for a very long time before surfacing for air. Blubber and a thick layer of fur keep seals warm.

Arctic seals, such as harp, hooded, and ringed seals, migrate in search of food and breeding grounds. Ringed seals are a polar bear's usual meal. Polar bears, arctic foxes, toothed whales, and sharks all hunt Arctic seals. Arctic seals live a dangerous life!

crabeater seal

Ice Holes

Seals create breathing holes in the ice by chewing with their teeth, scratching with their claws, and bashing with their heads.

Like Arctic seals, Antarctic seals travel in search of food and good breeding grounds. They have been known to visit the islands and continents close to Antarctica. Some important Antarctic seals include the leopard, Weddell, and crabeater seals. Like Arctic seals, the seals of the Antarctic are hunted by both sharks and toothed whales.

young ringed seal

Birds

Both the Arctic and the Antarctic are hosts to large populations of birds.

The snowy owl lives year-round on the tundra grasslands. Its white winter coat turns a spotted brown during summer. It has excellent sight and hearing. Snowy owls like to swoop down silently to catch rodents.

Unlike the snowy owl, the Arctic tern migrates more than twenty thousand miles every year! Arctic terns form communities of about fifty birds.

The wingspan of a snowy owl extends up to five feet across.

Arctic tern

Arctic terns rarely stop flying. They swoop down from the sky to catch fish and flying insects.

Most albatrosses live in the Antarctic, but some species are found in the Arctic. The albatross is one of the largest flying birds in the world. It spends most of its life at sea but returns to land in the summer to breed.

The auk belongs to a family of Arctic seabirds that includes puffins and razorbills. Auks and penguins look very similar. Unlike penguins, however, auks live in the Arctic and can fly. Auks are also very good swimmers. They snatch small fish, crustaceans, and mollusks from the water.

Auks can fly very fast, despite their short wings.

Caribou

Caribou are large mammals. They range across the Arctic tundra. Both male and female caribou grow antlers. Male caribou are called bulls. Their antlers can grow to be four feet across. The bull uses his antlers to attract female caribou and fight other bulls.

It only takes newborn caribou about an hour and a half to learn how to run! Soon after it is born, a caribou is running with the herds.

Caribou Moss

Caribou moss is a lichen. It is the caribou's most important winter food. Caribou smell caribou moss through the snow. They dig down deep to get to it.

Newborn caribou learn to walk and run almost immediately so that they can join the migrating herds.

Caribou populations migrate great distances across the tundra in search of good grazing land. In the spring and summer, they eat grasses and flowering plants. In the winter they survive on lichens. Caribou hooves are shaped perfectly for digging into the snow. Their hairs have a special structure that traps air and keeps them warm. Caribou are very strong swimmers. They paddle across rivers and the cold waters of the Arctic Ocean.

Arctic Wolves

Arctic wolves live on the North American tundra. They also live in northern Greenland and on islands close to the North Pole. Arctic wolves are smaller than most other wolves. Adults are only about three feet long. They have long, thick, white fur that insulates them from the harsh Arctic temperatures.

Like other wolves, Arctic wolves live and hunt in small communities called packs. About six wolves make up a pack. Each pack has a huge territory. The pack roams its territory searching for caribou, hares, and other prey.

Wolf Senses

Wolves are known for their excellent hearing, keen eyesight, and strong sense of smell. A wolf's senses are critical to its success as a hunter.

The fur of Arctic wolves remains white year-round.

Arctic wolves run very fast and have keen senses. Their teeth are long and sharp. A pack of Arctic wolves will often kill a much larger animal, such as a musk ox. They wait for a musk ox herd to leave a younger and weaker calf exposed. Then they attack. A pack of wolves can live off a musk ox for an entire week.

The female arctic wolf leaves the pack to find a den in late spring. She gives birth to between two and four pups. Arctic wolf pups are deaf and blind at birth. They depend on the pack totally for food and protection. After a year the pups can hunt for themselves.

Glossary

baleen   bony plates attached to the jaws of certain whales. Hairlike bristles fringe the plates and sieve food

blowhole   the hole on the top of a whale's head through which it breathes

blubber   thick, insulating layers of fat under the skin of many animals inhabiting the Arctic and the Antarctic

krill   small crustaceans in the ocean, similar to shrimp

lichen   a combination of fungus and algae growing together in a symbiotic relationship on rocks or tree trunks

permafrost   soil in the Arctic regions that has been frozen continuously for a very long time

predator   an animal that hunts another animal for food

regurgitate   to spit up partially digested food into the mouth of one's young